Personality Development through Positive Thinking

Personality Development through Positive Thinking

Amit Abraham

STERLING PAPERBACKS
An imprint of
Sterling Publishers (P) Ltd.
A-59, Okhla Industrial Area, Phase-II,
New Delhi-110020.
Tel: 26387070, 26386209; Fax: 91-11-26383788
E-mail: mail@sterlingpublishers.com
www.sterlingpublishers.com

Personality Development through Positive Thinking
© 2004, Sterling Publishers Private Limited
ISBN 978 81 207 5570 3
Reprint 2005, 2006, 2007, 2009, 2010, 2011, 2013

All rights are reserved.
No part of this publication may be reproduced, stored in a retrieval system or transmitted, in any form or by any means, mechanical, photocopying, recording or otherwise, without prior written permission of the original publisher.

Printed in India
Printed and Published by Sterling Publishers Pvt. Ltd.,
New Delhi-110 020.

CONTENTS

Preface	9
Acknowledgements	13
Dynamics of Personality Development	15
Importance of Mental Health	28
Dynamics of Positive Thinking	38
Perceiving Others – Impression Formation	43
Your Self-Esteem	54
Knowing Your Attitude	58
Self-Monitoring	69
Achiever's Profile – Do You Have It in You?	77
How Positively Do You Think?	86

*We may become the makers of our fate
when we have ceased to pose as its prophets*

Preface

I know that you know but you do not know that you really do not know – get to know your 'self'

While reading this book each one of you will say "I know". No one knows himself better than the individual himself but how truthful are you about yourself? The biggest liar is the one who lies to himself. Do you really think you are the individual you know? Think and then think about what you have thought. Is it what you really thought? Ask your conscience because in this world there is nothing more honest and sincere than one's conscience.

The two great movers of the human mind are the desire of good and the fear of evil. One should have a desire to be good and do well. Desire is the key to motivation. It is the key to develop a healthy personality and a positive attitude towards oneself and others.

Let us begin by creating a desire to be good, to feel good about ourselves and others and a desire to analyse ourselves honestly. The gradual development of this attitude will surely help you take a big leap towards personality development.

I hope that step-by-step browsing through this book will be an enlightening source for you to know your *self* better. It will help you to think and move in the positive direction and your personality will gradually but surely develop. However, one thing is important and that is an honest self-assessment from time to time. This assessment will give you the requisite feedback, necessary at every step and at all stages for personality development. You will find various scales in this book to help you test yourself and know yourself better.

As mentioned earlier this book is the outcome of my personal philosophy of positive thinking woven around psychosocial concepts applicable for personality development and growth. It is not important whether you agree or disagree with the concepts propounded, as you have the right to disagree. For me it is your thinking and not mine that is finally important.

About the book

A journey of a thousand miles must begin with a single step

This book is not about winning. It is also not about winners or success. It is about individuals who wish to achieve perfection in their relationships with themselves and others. It is about individuals pitted against themselves striving to be better individuals. It is about knowing oneself. It is about feeling better and thinking better. It is about one's attitudes and beliefs. In short, it is about the dynamics of positive thinking and personality development.

I know it is difficult to be the individuals we want to be, but it is not impossible. Thus it is significant that we think positive about ourselves and develop a high self-esteem. Everything is possible if sincere efforts are put in to achieve our goals. This book will guide you through each step. It will try to tell you and help you gauge positive and negative points. You will find various scales to help you approximately measure and find out the individual that you are. This will help you understand yourself better.

However, it is well said that forty people can take a horse to the well but they cannot make it drink. Ultimately it is your effort and your thinking that will change you.

I know many things are not possible in all situations. Our behaviours are largely governed by our assessment of the immediate situation and circumstances. We are humans and simply cannot be perfect in all respects. However we can strive for near perfection. I personally wish you all the best to go ahead and start thinking positive.

You can always e-mail your queries to me at:
amitabraham@sancharnet.in or
samvaidhna@hotmail.com.
I will be glad to help by offering you advice.

Dr Amit Abraham

Acknowledgements

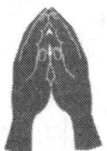

*Life can only be understood backwards;
but it must be lived forward*

First and foremost I would like to thank all those people who have been bad and mean to me. It was because of their wickedness that I became aware of the realities of life. Many people had been unjust to me and I did not know whom to trust. Hence I learnt to trust myself. It was out of this trust that I developed my philosophy of positive thought. I saw good in their bad. It gave me the strength from within to seek good out of evil. It helped me grow into a stronger individual from within. With each blow of theirs I emerged triumphant. I realised my weaknesses and worked on them. A well deserved thanks to all of them.

I am especially grateful to one *'big'* person who always wants to be labelled 'BIG' for creating a negative yet conducive environment and which enabled me to put my decades of thinking together and key it into my computer's hard disk.

Dr Malva Pope, Reader in the Department of English, has critically reviewed this book and her esteemed suggestions have been incorporated wherever possible. Thanks for being positively critical.

Ms Swati Sehgal who took pains to edit the book and gave positive suggestions for its improvement.

The publishers need to be thanked for the trust they showed in me by accepting to publish this book.

My better half, Dr Lisy, deserves the greatest acknowledgment for being the perfect wife one could ever wish for. From her I picked up many a fine thread for positive thought.

My daughter Swarnim, who is my strength and weakness too, has taught me the art of being appreciated by others. She surely is a charmer. To her I dedicate this piece of work.

Dr Amit Abraham

Dynamics of Personality Development

This world will not be a good place for any of us to live unless we make it a good place for all of us to live in

Personality can be defined as the deeply ingrained and relatively enduring patterns of thought, feeling and behaviour. Personality usually refers to that which is unique about a person, the characteristics that distinguish him or her from other people. Thoughts, emotions and behaviour as such do not constitute a personality, which is rather the disposition that underlie these elements. Personality implies predictability about how a person will act or react under different circumstances.

Theorists emphasise on different aspects of personality and disagree about its organisation, development and manifestation in behaviour. One of the most influential theoretical systems is the Psychoanalytic Theory of Sigmund Freud and his followers. Freud believed that unconscious processes direct a great part of a person's behaviour. Although a person is unaware of these impulses and drives, they strive to assert themselves. Another influential theory of personality is derived from Behaviourism. This view, represented by thinkers such as the American psychologist B. F. Skinner, places primary emphasis on learning. Skinner sees human behaviour as determined largely by its consequences. If rewarded, behaviour recurs; if punished, it is less likely to recur.

Formation and development
Heredity and environment interact to form personality. Right from birth, infants differ widely because of variables that are either inherited or result from conditions of pregnancy and birth. For example, some infants are more attentive than others, whereas some are more active. These differences can influence on how parents respond to the infant. Among the personality characteristics that are known to be at least partly determined by heredity, are intelligence and temperament; some forms of psychopathology are also in part hereditary.

In addition to the influences of heredity what happens to a developing child has a greater or lesser effect depending on when it happens. Many psychologists believe that critical periods exist in personality development. These are periods when an individual is more sensitive to a particular type of environmental event. During one period, for example, language ability changes most rapidly; during another, the capacity for guilt is most likely to be developing.

Most experts believe that a child's experiences in the family are crucial for personality development. How well the basic needs are met in infancy and during childhood can leave a permanent mark on personality. Children whose toilet training is started too early or carried out too rigidly, for example, may become defiant. Children learn behaviour appropriate to their sex by identifying with their same-sex parent; a warm relationship with that parent facilitates such learning. Children are also influenced by their siblings. Some authorities emphasise the role of social and cultural traditions in personality development.

Traditionally, psychologists hold that the traits of an individual combine to form a personality and that this personality shows great consistency over a period of time. Recently however, many psychologists have argued that traits exist only in the eye of the beholder and that a person's personality varies with the situation.

Implications

Traits vary with the situation and so, we can adapt and adjust ourselves with the environment and develop into healthy humans. The process of adaptation and adjustment is largely determined by the way we feel and look at things. It is our attitude that is responsible for such adaptations and adjustments. We have to think that all things, good or bad, have their positive side and should learn to take advantage of them. We can alter ourselves and perform tailor-made roles for our psychological and social benefits. So let us go ahead and do it.

Know yourself better

There are many personality tests measuring various dimensions of personality. It is not possible here to measure all dimensions of your personality, hence, a simplified measure of personality type has been developed to help you identify yourself in terms of types. Further ahead, you will come across various measures that will help you understand yourself much better.

The author has developed the following scales for the assessment of the personality type. It is based on the archetypal model of personality. According to this model, individuals can be classified into six categories. These are explained in detail after the assessment of personality type. Find your type.

Read each statement and respond as per what you feel — strong agreement/ agreement/ undecidedness/ disagreement/ strong disagreement with the statement. Be very honest and truthful to yourself.

A

1. I possess good motor coordination skills.
   Strongly agree/Agree/Undecided/Disagree/Strongly disagree
2. I have problems in communicating with people.
   Strongly agree/Agree/Undecided/Disagree/Strongly disagree
3. I cannot get along well with the group.
   Strongly agree/Agree/Undecided/Disagree/Strongly disagree
4. I do not feel comfortable in social gatherings.
   Strongly agree/Agree/Undecided/Disagree/Strongly disagree

5. I perceive myself as mechanically inclined.
   Strongly agree/Agree/Undecided/Disagree/Strongly disagree
6. I prefer concrete to abstract problems.
   Strongly agree/Agree/Undecided/Disagree/Strongly disagree
7. I have conventional goals, both political and economical.
   Strongly agree/Agree/Undecided/Disagree/Strongly disagree
8. I rarely perform well in the arts.
   Strongly agree/Agree/Undecided/Disagree/Strongly disagree
9. I rarely perform well in the sciences.
   Strongly agree/Agree/Undecided/Disagree/Strongly disagree
10. I possess very good verbal skills.
    Strongly agree/Agree/Undecided/Disagree/Strongly disagree

B

1. I have a strong scientific orientation.
   Strongly agree/Agree/Undecided/Disagree/Strongly disagree
2. I am task oriented.
   Strongly agree/Agree/Undecided/Disagree/Strongly disagree
3. I am introspective.
   Strongly agree/Agree/Undecided/Disagree/Strongly disagree

4. I am social.
   Strongly agree/Agree/Undecided/Disagree/Strongly disagree
5. I prefer to solve problems in a theoretical way.
   Strongly agree/Agree/Undecided/Disagree/Strongly disagree
6. I have a great need to understand the physical world.
   Strongly agree/Agree/Undecided/Disagree/Strongly disagree
7. I enjoy doing ambiguous tasks.
   Strongly agree/Agree/Undecided/Disagree/Strongly disagree
8. I prefer to work independently.
   Strongly agree/Agree/Undecided/Disagree/Strongly disagree
9. I am confident of my scholarly and intellectual activities.
   Strongly agree/Agree/Undecided/Disagree/Strongly disagree
10. I usually perceive myself as lacking in persuasive abilities.
    Strongly agree/Agree/Undecided/Disagree/Strongly disagree

C

1. I prefer free unstructured situations with maximum opportunity for self-expression.
   Strongly agree/Agree/Undecided/Disagree/Strongly disagree
2. I am asocial and have less ego problems.
   Strongly agree/Agree/Undecided/Disagree/Strongly disagree

3. I have a greater need for individual expression.
   Strongly agree/Agree/Undecided/Disagree/Strongly disagree
4. I am impulsive.
   Strongly agree/Agree/Undecided/Disagree/Strongly disagree
5. I am creative especially in the field of art and music.
   Strongly agree/Agree/Undecided/Disagree/Strongly disagree
6. I avoid highly structured problems or physical activity.
   Strongly agree/Agree/Undecided/Disagree/Strongly disagree
7. I see myself as original.
   Strongly agree/Agree/Undecided/Disagree/Strongly disagree
8. I see myself as non-confirming.
   Strongly agree/Agree/Undecided/Disagree/Strongly disagree
9. I am introvert.
   Strongly agree/Agree/Undecided/Disagree/Strongly disagree
10. I see myself as independent.
    Strongly agree/Agree/Undecided/Disagree/Strongly disagree

D

1. I will make a good sales executive.
   Strongly agree/Agree/Undecided/Disagree/Strongly disagree

2. I am dominating and leading.
   Strongly agree/Agree/Undecided/Disagree/Strongly disagree
3. I have a strong drive to attain goals.
   Strongly agree/Agree/Undecided/Disagree/Strongly disagree
4. I have a strong drive to attain economic goals.
   Strongly agree/Agree/Undecided/Disagree/Strongly disagree
5. I tend to avoid work situations requiring long periods of intellectual efforts.
   Strongly agree/Agree/Undecided/Disagree/Strongly disagree
6. I prefer ambiguous social tasks.
   Strongly agree/Agree/Undecided/Disagree/Strongly disagree
7. I have a great concern for power, status and leadership.
   Strongly agree/Agree/Undecided/Disagree/Strongly disagree
8. I am very aggressive.
   Strongly agree/Agree/Undecided/Disagree/Strongly disagree
9. I am very popular within the group.
   Strongly agree/Agree/Undecided/Disagree/Strongly disagree
10. I have strong confidence in my abilities.
    Strongly agree/Agree/Undecided/Disagree/Strongly disagree

E

1. I have many friends.
   Strongly agree/Agree/Undecided/Disagree/Strongly disagree
2. I take up responsibilities easily.
   Strongly agree/Agree/Undecided/Disagree/Strongly disagree
3. I care for all my fellow human beings.
   Strongly agree/Agree/Undecided/Disagree/Strongly disagree
4. I say my prayers daily.
   Strongly agree/Agree/Undecided/Disagree/Strongly disagree
5. I am happier working with a group.
   Strongly agree/Agree/Undecided/Disagree/Strongly disagree
6. I have the knack for oration/oratory.
   Strongly agree/Agree/Undecided/Disagree/Strongly disagree
7. I do not like to boggle my brains trying to solve puzzles.
   Strongly agree/Agree/Undecided/Disagree/Strongly disagree
8. I prefer to solve problems through feelings and interpersonal manipulation of others.
   Strongly agree/Agree/Undecided/Disagree/Strongly disagree
9. I enjoy indulging in activities that involve informing, curing, developing and enlightening others.
   Strongly agree/Agree/Undecided/Disagree/Strongly disagree

10. I perceive myself as understanding, idealistic and helpful.
    Strongly agree/Agree/Undecided/Disagree/Strongly disagree.

F

1. I prefer well-ordered environment.
   Strongly agree/Agree/Undecided/Disagree/Strongly disagree
2. I prefer systematic verbal and numerical activities.
   Strongly agree/Agree/Undecided/Disagree/Strongly disagree
3. I like conforming and subordinate roles.
   Strongly agree/Agree/Undecided/Disagree/Strongly disagree
4. I am effective at well-structured tasks.
   Strongly agree/Agree/Undecided/Disagree/Strongly disagree.
5. I avoid ambiguous situations involving interpersonal relationships.
   Strongly agree/Agree/Undecided/Disagree/Strongly disagree.
6. I am obedient, calm, orderly and practical.
   Strongly agree/Agree/Undecided/Disagree/Strongly disagree.
7. I identify with power and value.
   Strongly agree/Agree/Undecided/Disagree/Strongly disagree.
8. I identify with status.
   Strongly agree/Agree/Undecided/Disagree/Strongly disagree.

9. I identify with material possessions.
    Strongly agree/Agree/Undecided/Disagree/Strongly disagree.
10. I avoid ambiguous situations involving physical skills.
    Strongly agree/Agree/Undecided/Disagree/Strongly disagree.

After you have marked your responses take each section separately and assign 5 points to *strongly agree*; 4 points to *agree*; 3 points to *undecided*; 2 points to *disagree* and 1 point to *strongly disagree*. Total your score for each of the six sections separately. You will thus have a total score for A, B, C, D, E and F. Arrange the scores in descending order (highest score first, then next and so on). This gives you your personality type order. Check against the description you fit into as per your alphabetical hierarchy.

A: You are the **realistic type** and possess good motor coordination skills but lack verbal and interpersonal skills. You may at times be feeling uncomfortable in social settings. You perceive yourself mechanically inclined and prefer concrete to abstract problems. You have conventional political and economical goals. You rarely perform creatively in the arts or sciences but like to build things with tools. Appropriate careers for you are: fishery and wildlife specialist, tool designer, mechanic, engineer, electrician and crane operator.

B: You are the **investigative type**. You have a strong scientific orientation and are usually task oriented, introspective and asocial. You prefer to think more rather than practically handling your problems. You have a great need to understand the physical world. You enjoy ambiguous tasks, prefer to work all by yourself and usually perceive yourself as lacking in persuasive abilities. You are confident of your scholarly and intellectual abilities. You have unconventional values and attitudes. The careers best suited are: astronomer, biologist, chemist, technical writer, zoologist and psychologist.

C: You are the **artistic type**. You prefer unstructured situations with maximum opportunity for self-expression. You are introspective and not very social and have less ego problems. You have a greater need for individual expression as well as a greater tendency to impulsive behaviour. You generally avoid highly structured problems or physical activity and see yourself as original, intuitive, creative, nonconforming, introspective and independent. The careers most suitable include those of an artist, composer, writer, musician, stage director and symphony conductor.

D: You are the **enterprising type**. You possess good verbal skills most suitable for selling. You have a dominating nature and have strong leadership traits. You have a strong drive to attain organisational goals and economic gains. You generally tend to avoid work situations requiring long periods of intellectual efforts. You prefer ambiguous social tasks and have a great concern for power, status and leadership. You see yourself as aggressive, popular, self-confident, cheerful and social. You have a high energy level. Suitable careers are those of business executive, political campaign manager, real estate, sales, stock and bond sales, television producer and retail merchandising.

E: You are the **social type**. You are very social and responsible, humanistic and often religious too. You like to work in groups and possess good verbal and interpersonal skills. However, you avoid solving intellectual problems, physical exertion and highly ordered social activities. You prefer to solve problems through feelings and interpersonal manipulation of others. You enjoy activities that involve informing, curing, developing or enlightening others. You perceive yourself as understanding, idealistic and helpful. Careers best suited for you include those of a social worker, missionary, teacher, marriage counsellor and speech therapist.

F: You are the **conventional type**. You prefer well-ordered environments and are inclined to systematic verbal and numerical activities. You readily go with the group and do not mind doing subordinate roles. You are very efficient when tasks are well-defined and structured and tend to avoid ambiguous situations involving interpersonal relationships or physical tasks. You are very obedient, calm, orderly and practical. You identify with power, status, material possessions and value. Careers best suited for you are that of an auditor, statistician, cost analyst, accountant, tax specialist and banker.

Importance of Mental Health

The least of things with a meaning is worth more in life than the greatest of things without it

For persons to develop into healthy humans it is necessary that they have a good mental health. Mental health means a psychological state of well-being, characterised by continuing personal growth, a sense of purpose in life, self-acceptance and positive relations with others.

Elements of mental health

Psychologists have identified numerous distinct dimensions of mental health which include *self-acceptance* or *self-esteem*, characterised by a positive evaluation of oneself and one's past experiences; personal growth reflected in one's sense of continued psychological growth and development; a sense that one's life has purpose and meaning; positive relations with others; environmental mastery, the capacity to manage effectively in the surrounding world; and autonomy, a sense of self-determination and the ability to control one's own life. Self-acceptance, relation with others, environmental mastery and autonomy usually improves as a person ages and gains experiences in life. However, many people find that their personal growth and sense of purpose in life begins to decline in midlife.

Some psychologists regard mental health as the ability to maintain a balance between positive and negative emotions, such as elation and sadness. In this view, a person who displays emotional extremes in either direction is not well adjusted. Other psychologists emphasise the role of one's environment in influencing well-being. This perspective sees a reflection of mental health in a person's overall happiness in various domains of life, such as social relationships, work and community life.

Factors that have an influence on mental health

A number of different aspects of life can influence mental health. These areas are working life, family life and one's social role in the community. Negative experiences in these areas, such as an unreasonable boss or a turbulent family life, can reduce one's overall sense of well-being.

Another important influence on mental health is *stress*. In general, people experience stress when the demands placed on them exceed the resources they have to meet those demands. Significant sources of stress include major life events, such as divorce, death of a spouse, loss of a job and illness in the family. These events can overwhelm a person's ability to cope and function effectively. In addition, one source of stress may lead to another, as when financial hardships follow a loss of job. People who experience unusually traumatic events, such as rape and natural disasters, may develop post-traumatic stress disorder.

People may experience chronic stress when confronted with a continuing set of demands that reduce their ability to function. Examples of such demands include working long hours under difficult circumstances and caring for a chronically-ill relative. Economic hardship, unemployment and poverty can also produce chronic stress and undermine mental health.

Some studies suggest that genetic factors may partly determine one's level of happiness and mental health. People seem to display a characteristic level of well-being, with some people usually feeling happy and others typically feeling sad or unhappy. Researchers have found that although people's moods change in response to both positive and negative events, the effect wears off over a period of time. For example, people who win a lottery or receive an unexpected promotion may feel happier at first, but with time they return to their former characteristic level of mental health. Research also suggests that one's genetic make-up, that is, the genes inherited from one's parents explains more than half of the differences in people's characteristic mood levels. Genes may also partly determine the range of ups and downs that people feel, ranging from large mood swings to remaining stable from day-to-day.

How mentally healthy are you?

The following scale is designed by the author to measure approximately the level of your mental health. Respond to each statement in accordance with your feelings with full truthfulness. Unless and until you know yourself you cannot assess properly. Remember that truth is the key to your personality development.

1. I am not confident about my abilities.
   Always/Most of the time/Sometime/Never
2. Small problems easily upset me.
   Always/Most of the time/Sometime/Never
3. I am worried about my future.
   Always/Most of the time/Sometime/Never
4. I lack the ability to take decisions.
   Always/Most of the time/Sometime/Never
5. I have mood fluctuations.
   Always/Most of the time/Sometime/Never
6. I suffer from feelings of insecurity.
   Always/Most of the time/Sometime/Never
7. Others have to help me make decisions.
   Always/Most of the time/Sometime/Never
8. Even when in a group I do not feel secure.
   Always/Most of the time/Sometime/Never
9. I feel that I am losing self-respect.
   Always/Most of the time/Sometime/Never
10. I cannot reach a decision even when I want to do a particular thing.
    Always/Most of the time/Sometime/Never
11. I have a feeling that some calamities may occur with me.
    Always/Most of the time/Sometime/Never

12. I cannot finish tasks in one go.
    Always/Most of the time/Sometime/Never
13. I am unable to solve my problems myself.
    Always/Most of the time/Sometime/Never
14. I feel that my future is not well-planned and defined.
    Always/Most of the time/Sometime/Never
15. I shirk away from responsibilities.
    Always/Most of the time/Sometime/Never
16. I am not able to take quick decisions on any matter.
    Always/Most of the time/Sometime/Never
17. I feel that this world is very hostile.
    Always/Most of the time/Sometime/Never
18. I need a conducive work environment.
    Always/Most of the time/Sometime/Never
19. I am unsatisfied with my life.
    Always/Most of the time/Sometime/Never
20. I become hopeless when I fail in any task.
    Always/Most of the time/Sometime/Never
21. I do not get along well with the people in my locality.
    Always/Most of the time/Sometime/Never
22. I feel depressed and dejected. *Always/Most of the time/Sometime/Never*
23. I suffer from feelings of inferiority.
    Always/Most of the time/Sometime/Never
24. I am enraged even by the slightest unfavourable talk.
    Always/Most of the time/Sometime/Never
25. I feel my life is a burden for others in my family.
    Always/Most of the time/Sometime/Never
26. Minor difficulties disappoint me.
    Always/Most of the time/Sometime/Never

27. I lack concentration while working.
    Always/Most of the time/Sometime/Never
28. I build castles in the air.
    Always/Most of the time/Sometime/Never
29. I do not have a flexible approach.
    Always/Most of the time/Sometime/Never
30. In adverse circumstances I act without keeping real facts in view.
    Always/Most of the time/Sometime/Never

After you have marked your responses give 1 point to every *Always* you have ticked; 2 points to every *Most of the time*; 3 points to *Sometimes* and 4 points to *Never*. Total up the points obtained. If you score between 91-120 you have a **very good** mental health. If your score lies between 61-90 your mental health is **good** or **average**. Between 31-60 it is **poor**. Between 0-30 it is **very poor**.

The way to be mentally healthy

If you have a poor or very poor mental health do not worry. Try out the following:

- **Develop within you adequate feelings of security**. Identify the insecurities within and around you. Some may be real and most of them imaginary. Work out solutions for the real ones and forget the unreal ones. Insecurities generally arise due to lack of faith in us. We feel inadequate in handling the difficult situations in life. We begin to worry about our future. We give up our struggles against odds and quit. Do not quit. Handle the present and future will take care of itself.

- **Do honest and adequate self-evaluation.** Know yourself. Identify your strengths and accept your weaknesses. Accepting and then overcoming your weaknesses will strengthen you. You will have a stronger reservoir.
- **Develop adequate spontaneity and emotionality.** You should be spontaneous in all your doings. Do not wait for a push or pull. Charge your energies and remain fully charged. Be emotionally warm to others because what you sow, so shall you reap. Receiving emotional warmth from others is good for your mental health.
- **Maintain efficient contact with reality.** Diana Hayden quoted in the Miss Universe pageant "In dreams begin realities." Even if you are a dreamer then let your dreams be positively oriented so that you can turn them into realities. Learn to live in this world and not outside it.
- **Have adequate bodily desires and the ability to gratify them.** Man surely cannot live by bread alone. He needs to fulfil his other biological needs as well and have the ability to do so. Eat, drink, sleep and be merry. You should eat and sleep adequately. But every one of us does not get to fulfil these desires at the same price. Many have to pay heavily for adequate food and sleep. If you are one of them then work out your schedule so that you can afford this luxury. It will surely benefit you. "A healthy mind is a healthy body", is a very old saying.

- **Have adequate self-knowledge**. Know thy self and health will follow. Many of us are ignorant about ourselves. We tend to either underestimate or overestimate ourselves. Both have their disadvantages. We are what we are and not what we think we are. However, we should always think positively about ourselves.
- **Have an integrated and consistent personality**. We have to put ourselves together. We have to have consistency in thought and action. Avoid having a split personality. Remember united you stand and divided you fall. The same applies for personality. A well-integrated and consistent individual with a balanced mind will always be strong and mentally healthy.
- **Have adequate life goals**. A life without a motive is virtually a life without a purpose. You are in this world with some purpose. Define your aims and objectives in life. Set your goals and go out to achieve them. See the pleasure that achievement brings. It gives you happiness and joy that are the key to a good mental health.
- **Learn from experiences**. A burnt child dreads the fire but as he grows he also learns the positive utilities of fire. We all have good as well as bad experiences in life, and we learn from both. Bad experiences teach us how to constantly have good ones. Surely there is no better a teacher in this world than experience.

- **Develop the ability to satisfy the requirements of the group**. Man is a social animal who is constantly in active interaction with other individuals. We give and we receive. We have to go along with the norms and fulfil social requirements of the society. We have to resonate in consonance to avoid dissonance.

Maintaining mental health

The ability to cope with adversity can be crucial for the mental health of the individual. *Coping* means successfully dealing with problems that arise in life. People differ substantially in the way they cope with adversity. Some people engage in *emotion-focused coping*, a strategy that focuses on managing one's emotions. Examples of this coping strategy include distracting one's attention from the problem, denying the problem, venting one's emotions or sharing emotions with others. A second form of coping, *problem-focused coping*, involves efforts to reduce stress by solving the problem. People who use this strategy take active steps to overcome the problem, such as seeing a counsellor to repair a relationship or looking for a new job in response to problems at work. They may also seek advice from friends and family members.

Some people use coping skills more effectively than others. However, research has shown that people can learn new coping skills. For example, counsellors can teach children how to handle difficulties in school. Adults can be taught skills to cope with stressful events in life, such as loss of a job and divorce. Teaching coping skills to people before they encounter adversity, or early in the stages of a crisis, appears to be an effective method of preventing poor mental health. Learning effective coping strategies also directly improves mental health by improving one's sense of mastery and self-esteem.

Social support from friends and family members also promotes good mental health. Friends respond with concern, empathy and advice to a person facing difficulties or loss. They boost confidence and self-esteem by offering reassurances and compliments. Self-help groups provide support by enabling people with similar problems to share their experiences and emotions. Conversely, research has shown that negative social interactions, such as constant criticism and belittlement from other people, can undermine mental health.

Another way of maintaining good mental health is by getting involved in physical activities. For example, research has shown that regular aerobic exercise helps to boost self-esteem, relieve depression and improve concentration. Relaxation techniques, such as deep breathing and meditation, also help to combat the effects of stress.

Dynamics of Positive Thinking

If you do not know where you are going, you will probably end up somewhere else

Thinking is defined as the action of one's mind to produce thoughts. These thoughts can either be negative or positive. Positive thoughts are directed towards problem-solving behaviour. Negative thoughts find expression in excuses for the failure or in trying to avoid problem-solving behaviour. One who thinks in the negative direction is called a *pessimist* while one who thinks in the positive direction an *optimist*.

Thoughts range between two extremes – *autistic* and *realistic*. Autistic thinking is determined primarily by our own needs, wishes and feelings, whereas realistic thinking is determined largely by the requirements of the objective situation. Autistic thinking may frequently be indulged in for self-gratification without considering the reality. This type of thinking is the more primitive mode of thinking, characteristic of the unconscious. It manifests itself most clearly in dreams, but presumably exists as an undercurrent in waking life as well. The jumbled thoughts of the mentally challenged and of normal people, under the influence of certain drugs, illustrate its activity: ideas are guided solely by a desire for immediate wish fulfilment – with no concern for logic, morality, time sequence, casual connections or the demands of external reality. Thinking at this level obeys the *pleasure principle* – the seeking of pleasure and the avoidance of pain. Doubt, uncertainty and contradictions have no place in autistic thinking.

Realistic thinking, on the other hand tends to be productive – to be directed towards action or the solution of a problem. This type of thinking is the characteristic mode of preconscious and conscious. Thinking at this level obeys the *reality principle* – the regulation and control of behaviour according to the demands of the outside world. Anticipation of probable changes in the environment and of consequences of acts leads to the ability to delay gratification by relinquishing immediate satisfaction in favour of a better-adjusted and more adaptive long-range plan of action.

To understand the basis of thinking it is essential to also know about the dynamics of behaviour. Behaviour refers to goal-directed patterns of reactions which can be observed objectively. It also refers to internal processes such as thinking and emotional reactions, which can be observed introspectively or inferred from external behaviour.

To understand and evaluate behaviour in its totality we have to break the entire process into its various components and establish a clear relationship among them and then only can we evaluate others and ourselves in a positive direction.

Goal-directed patterns of reactions or other external behaviour is the outcome of stimulation. This stimulation can either be from an external or internal source. The organism receives stimulation and emits a response. This response is his behaviour. Many processes are involved in this entire mechanism. First the stimulus is to be attended to and recognised, then perception occurs. Many laws and factors govern perception. The most important factor is our past experience which among others, includes our attitudes, beliefs and values. Together this makes our perception an apperception. Apperception means past experience plus present ones. Thus, the past and present both determine our perception and thereby our behaviour.

Our thinking about others and ourselves is influenced by *empathy*. Empathy means the understanding and sharing of another person's emotional experience in a particular situation. In other words, empathy is the ability to put one's self in another's place to understand the other person's views and feelings (thought). Where there is no empathy there is no positive thought for the other.

Motivation is another important aspect in behaviour. Any behaviour is guided by patterns of internal and external conditions. These complexes of internal and external conditions, called motives or drives, serve to direct the organism towards specific goals. Motivation, thus, answers the 'why' of behaviour. Behaviour can be directed towards or away from a goal depending on the type and kind of motivation. We think and then act in accordance with our thought.

Behaviour is finally the outcome of the product of an individual's intelligence. Intelligence is defined as the aggregate global capacity of an individual to act purposefully, to think rationally and to deal effectively with his environment. This definition needs to be broken down and examined in its components.

The first component that needs to be examined is *act purposefully*. This means that our behaviour should have a definite purpose and direction, ie it should have a motive. Most of us are not acting purposefully. We are acting mostly on the tune of others. Though man is born free but everywhere he is in chains. We have to free ourselves from bondage. We have to be free and think freely. Think and act with a positive attitude towards life. This is the first step towards positive thinking.

The second component to be examined is *think rationally*. This means having reason and understanding. Reason and understanding are very essential for positive thinking. Most of us are not thinking reasonably. Our thoughts are centred around and influenced by what others think about us. We live, think and act for others. The psychology of person perception says that we view the world through our perceptive glasses, ie we view others and evaluate them with the point of reference being ourselves. Thus we evaluate others according to what we think about ourselves. Now if we have positive thoughts about ourselves it will help us in thinking more rationally. It will help develop one's reasoning and understanding much better.

The third component is *deal effectively with the environment*. Effective dealing means efficient manipulation of the environment for psychological, social and economic well-being. However, this is possible only when one is confident about his abilities and potentials. This in turn comes from self-perception. It is important that we do not underestimate our abilities and potentials or those of others. We all have our plus and minus points. All we have to do is think positively about ourselves, our abilities and potentials, as well as accept our weaknesses and try to overcome them. This will surely work as magic.

Perceiving Others – Impression Formation

All our knowledge has its origins in our perceptions

Knowing others is as important as knowing yourself. Your thinking and personality development is largely influenced by the world around you. How do we come to know about other people? Our first impression of others is initially based on the information we hear about them and, in some instances, the inferences we make about the cause for their behaviour. When we have only a limited amount of information available we tend to fill in the gaps to arrive at a fairly complete and comprehensive image of the individual in question.

Forming impressions of other people is probably so natural and habitual that everyone does it, consciously or unconsciously. Impression formation is a process by which information about others is converted into more or less enduring cognitions or thoughts about them. When we first meet someone we have access to considerable information — how the person looks and what he or she does and says. According to one point of view, we are not overwhelmed by the abundance of this information because we are able to group it into categories that predict things of importance to us. These categories and their perceived interrelationships form the basic cognitive framework by which we understand others. The linkages among these categories will determine what predictions we make about someone when we have only limited information. If, for example, you think people who wear glasses are intelligent, then whenever you meet a stranger wearing glasses, you will be disposed to believe that he or she is highly intelligent. All categories are related to some other categories and unrelated to many more. In your mind, wearing glasses might also be related to 'timidness' but not to 'honesty' or 'sense of humour'. By generating predictors or expectations, we can efficiently interact with other people even when we possess only minimal information about them.

Of course there is no guarantee that different people will categorise a given piece of information in the same way. You have probably had the experience of finding that your first impression of a person differs markedly from that of your friends. There is evidence that people vary in the way they tend to evaluate others on first meeting them. One such difference is that some people are predisposed to like everyone they meet. They may focus on the desirable characteristics of others and search for evidence that people possess certain favourable traits. Others have a tendency to dislike people on their first meeting and may try to discover the existence of undesirable characteristics.

The categories we use and their assumed interrelationships constitute our template or framework for understanding the world in which we live. This framework, in essence, is our theory about how things are supposed to work.

For understanding other people, the category most frequently used is the *trait*. Traits are classification schemes for describing the behaviour of individuals. Our language provides us with many options for describing behaviour, such as assertive, friendly, punctual or talkative. Traits are a compelling set of categories used to describe, remember and communicate our own and other person's behaviour. Traits are also perceived to be interrelated; they seem to occur in clusters. You might, for example, assume that people who are assertive are also ambitious or that intelligent people are also industrious. This assumed relationship among traits is called ***implicit personality theory***, a name that underscores how our own cognitive framework generates predictions about other people that go beyond the information available to us. Implicit personality theory helps us to simplify the information we receive in social interaction, colour the way we interpret events and guide our responses to other people.

When you meet someone, you observe that person and assume that he or she possesses a certain set of traits. To make this decision, you must make a global judgment about how favourable you feel towards the person. One procedure you might follow is to add the favourable traits together. You will have a more positive impression. If you think a person is both kind and honest, than if you think the person is simply kind. On the other hand, you might average these two pieces of information, in which case your impression would remain about the same – the average of the two favourable traits would be close to the value of each of them alone. The averaging model is probably closer to what you would actually do; except that it would not be quite simple. Instead, certain pieces of information would be seen as more important and thus would be weighted more heavily than others; your overall impression would represent a weighted average of the information you have about that person. One thing you would consider is the relevance of the information for the particular judgment you are making. You assign importance to different characteristics in assessing different persons. Information obtained first also seems to be weighted more heavily. Most people believe there is some value in making a good first impression, and research shows that such efforts are not wasted; a primacy effect does often occur in impression formation. Furthermore, we generally give more importance to information concerning negative traits than to information concerning positive traits that others might possess. Each of these factors affects the weight people give to various pieces of information, when forming an impression of another person.

Now how does one go about doing this evaluation work? A list of adjectives is given in *Table 1* with the help of which we can measure the tendency to evaluate others in a positive or negative fashion. Before reading further, check the 12 characteristics that concern you in evaluating others. (For the moment, ignore the letters that follow the traits.)

Table 1

Sincere (H)	Solemn (M)
Honest (H)	Proud (M)
Understanding (H)	Prudent (M)
Trustworthy (H)	Shrewd (M)
Intelligent (H)	Materialistic (M)
Open-minded (H)	Eccentric (M)
Friendly (H)	Boring (L)
Gentle (H)	Touchy (L)
Courteous (H)	Boastful (L)
Tactful (H)	Conceited (L)
Well-read (H)	Phoney (L)
Witty (H)	Childish (L)
Authoritative (M)	Nosey (L)
Self-possessed (M)	Snobbish (L)
Sceptical (M)	Hostile (L)
Forceful (M)	Finicky (L)
Conservative (M)	Stingy (L)
Nonchalant (M)	Complaining (L)

Now go back and count the number of **H's, M's,** and **L's** on the traits you checked. They stand for high, medium or low in likability. If you have a majority of **H's**, you probably tend to view people favourably on first meeting them. If most of the adjectives you checked are **L's**, you are likely to have unfavourable first impressions of others.

It has been found that certain personality variables may influence our initial evaluations of others. Individuals use different dimensions when they evaluate others. Their evaluations are based on their own motives, emotions, interests and personality make-up.

Another aspect that plays an important role in impression formation is **physical attractiveness**. Physical attractiveness is the combination of facial features, physique and grooming that is perceived as aesthetically appealing by members of a given culture at a given time period.

When we first meet someone, we are likely to notice his or her physical appearance before anything else. Considerable research has demonstrated that one just does that. We have a strong tendency to be favourably impressed by attractive people and to be less favourably impressed with those who are not so attractive. One thing we must keep in mind while discussing about physical attractiveness is that beauty is in the eyes of the beholder and that the criteria of physical attractiveness is gender specific.

A good deal of research reveals that we tend to like others who are similar to us. Why should this be so; there are many reasons. People strive for cognitive consistency among their attitudes and behaviour. People who agree on important matters will become attracted to each other because they satisfy one another's needs for consistency. We may also be attracted to others who are similar to us because we assume they will like us. And being liked can in turn produce liking for the would-be friend. When we perceive others as similar to us, it encourages us to expect more positive outcomes from interaction with them. Also, when we find others who hold similar attitudes, we are attracted to them because they validate our own.

However, the universal law of magnetism states that opposite poles attract. This law also holds true in the case of attractiveness. People with same personality traits 'rub us the wrong way', while we feel comfortable with those who have certain different traits. Research has indicated that complementary needs play in producing attraction. Stress here is laid on difference rather than similarities. Complementary needs refer to two different personality traits that are the counterparts of each other and that provide a sense of completeness when they are joined. They mutually supply each other's lack. Although the theory includes attraction between friends of the same or opposite sex, it is seen most clearly in the area of mate selection. We typically seek within the field of eligible mates a person who gives the greatest promise of providing us with the maximum gratification of our needs.

Many of our needs are met in a complementary manner. People who possess a strong desire for recognition may love and be loved by people who prefer to bask in the achievements of others. Within such relationships, each person finds his or her needs satisfied. People with a need to nurture/for nurturing – a need to sympathise with or help others in difficulty – find fulfilment with people having a need for succour – a need to be helped and taken care of. Dominant people find a complementary relationship with submissive people. Talkative people find themselves attracted to taciturn people. Sadists find a reciprocal sense of satisfaction and well-being with masochists. However, interpersonal attraction based on complementary needs depend upon the extent to which individuals gratify one another's social needs and fulfil the obligations of the role context in which the relationship exists.

Although the theory of complementary needs appears to find confirmation in everyday life, actual studies have produced mixed findings. While a number support the theory, others fail to confirm it. One problem is that some of our personality needs are complemented by similarity rather than by contrast. Thus a combination of similarity and contrast, in varying degree, plays an important role in interpersonal attraction.

Apart from outward beauty, **attribution** also plays an important role in determining our attractiveness. How we judge people when we first meet them has a lot to do with our initial feelings towards them.

To characterise other people in terms of certain traits, intentions or abilities requires us to make attributions or inferences about them. But we do not have access to the personal thoughts, motives or feelings of others, because of which we make inferences about these traits based on the behaviour we observe. By making such attributions from certain behaviours, we are able to increase our ability to predict how a person will behave in the future.

Attributions are important because the causes we attribute to the behaviour of others can influence our own behaviour as well. For example, suppose you arrive at a party and see an attractive woman/man sitting alone. In speculating about why that person is sitting alone, two possibilities may occur to you. The person concerned may not be knowing anyone else at the party and, being somewhat reserved, may be reluctant to initiate conversation with others. Or, she/he may simply be waiting for her/his date to arrive. If you settle on the first attribution, you may very well walk over and introduce yourself to that person. If you decide that the second attribution is more likely, then you may begin to look around for someone else irrespective of the physical appeal of that person.

One advantage of attribution is that it takes into account the situational factors involved. Attribution suggests that the situation a person is in can have an important effect on how the other person is perceived.

There are two types of attributions: *personal* or *internal* attributions and *environmental* or *external* attributions. Let us take an example to explain these. Suppose a stranger in a restaurant trips over an end table and spills your tea. If you view him as clumsy then this will be your personal attribution. But if you blame the furniture arrangement for this mishap, it will be an environmental attribution.

Several studies have found that people tend to make personal attributions for the undesirable behaviour of others and make environmental attributions for similar behaviour of their own. Conversely, people tend to make environmental attributions for the success of others and personal attributions for their own success. Thus if we get into an argument with someone, we assume that they are aggressive and hostile, and that we are forced by the situation to defend our position.

The attributions one makes can vary depending on certain personality characteristics. Individuals with high levels of self-esteem tend to follow the pattern described above. If they are successful on a particular task, they make personal attributions, and if they fail, they make environmental attributions. Individuals low in self-esteem tend to do just the opposite. It appears that those with low self-esteem cannot believe anything good about themselves, while those with high self-esteem cannot believe anything bad about themselves.

In the final analysis, we can say that the process by which we form impressions of others is an efficient indication of our reactions to others. Our impressions are grounded in our observations of others – their physical characteristics and their behaviour in particular settings. Our observations provide the information that is converted into meaningful inferences by our cognitive framework. At a minimum, this process involves placing the information into cognitive categories, which are related to other categories. We can, thus, make simple inferences from minimum data or combine rich sets of information into overall impressions. Under some circumstances, we can also make inferences about the cause of other people's behaviour as well as our own behaviour. Despite the smoothness by which the process works, it does not guarantee accuracy or comparability with other's observations. Each of us makes a personal contribution to the process because we may have different ways of categorising the information, individual aspects to our cognitive framework or some unique way of combining information. Nevertheless, *the end result of impression formation determines how we react to others and how we see ourselves.*

Your Self-Esteem

What matters today is not the difference between those who believe and those who do not believe, but the difference between those who care and those who do not

We can move towards self-actualisation only when our need for self-esteem is fulfilled. How are we to know if our need for self-esteem is fulfilled? We will have to pass through a measure for the same. We will have to find out if we have a high or low self-esteem.

Assessing your self-esteem level

The measure below is designed by the author to approximately measure your level of self-esteem. Respond in the positive or negative with full truthfulness to the statements given.
1. Most of the time I am mentally happy. *Yes/No*
2. I seldom have health problems, such as ulcers. *Yes/No*
3. I sleep well during the nights. *Yes/No*
4. I do not generally succumb to group pressure for the sake of conformity. *Yes/No*
5. I can handle difficult situations without the use of stimulants. *Yes/No*

6. I do not consume sedatives. *Yes/No*
7. I take up difficult tasks and see them successfully through. *Yes/No*
8. I have a happy go lucky attitude. *Yes/No*
9. I do not have many good things to say about myself. *Yes/No*
10. Most of the time some problem or the other is bothering me. *Yes/No*
11. I suffer from pangs of depression. *Yes/No*
12. I have a high level of anxiety. *Yes/No*
13. I easily go along with the group decisions even if I do not agree with them. *Yes/No*
14. At times I feel very insecure. *Yes/No*
15. I indulge in self-persecution. *Yes/No*
16. I feel most of the people do not like me. *Yes/No*

After you have marked your responses give 1 point each to *Yes* answer for questions 1-8 and 1 point each to *No* answer for questions 9-16. Then add the total. If you have scored between 0-4 you have a very **low self-esteem**. If your score is between 5-10 you are **average** on self-esteem and if your score is between 11-16 you have a **high self-esteem**.

Implications – review yourself

If you have scored high on self-esteem do not just move ahead to self-actualisation. If you are low on self-esteem do not worry. Actually, most people see themselves as better than average. This is true for nearly any subjective and socially desirable dimension. All of us have inferiority complexes and those who seem not to have such a complex are only pretending. We remember and justify our past actions in self-enhancing ways. We exhibit an inflated confidence in the accuracy of our beliefs and judgments. We overestimate how desirably we would act in situations where most people behave less than admirably. We are quicker to believe flattering descriptions of ourselves than unflattering ones, and we are impressed with psychological tests that make us look good. We shore up our self-image by overestimating how much others support our opinions and share our foibles by underestimating the commonality of our strengths.

Moreover, pride often leads to a fall. Self-serving perceptions underlie conflicts ranging from blaming others for marital discord to self-promoting ethnic snobbery. The fact is that all of us sometimes, and some of us most of the time, do feel inferior – especially when we compare ourselves with those who are a step or two higher on the ladder of status, grades, looks, income or agility. The deeper and more frequently we have such feelings, the more unhappy, even depressed, we are.

But for most people – 98 per cent, who at anytime are not suffering depression, thinking has a natural positive bias.

Self-affirming thinking is generally adaptive. To a point even our positive illusions are beneficial. They maintain our self-confidence, protect against anxiety and depression, and sustain our senses of well-being. Humans function best with modest self-enhancing illusions. It is rightly said – "Life is the art of being well-deceived."

To enhance our self-esteem we have to make an effort to think positively about ourselves. We have to believe that we have it in us. We have to groom ourselves to standards of excellence. People are not born great. If greatness is thrust upon people they still have to prove their capability. We all have to achieve this greatness. This greatness comes from within and it is the most powerful source. The potentials are there and they just need to be unfurled. So go ahead and tap it. It is all in you and all yours.

Knowing Your Attitude

This above all; to thine own self be true, And it must follow, as the night and day, Thou canst not then be false to any man

It is a well-known fact that attitudes *guide* behaviour and definitely play a prominent role in our personality make-up. We can *to an extent* predict a person's behaviour if we know his attitude. But the ways in which attitudes, and other influences effect behaviour have to be considered very carefully.

An attitude is a relatively stable organisation of beliefs, feelings and tendencies towards something or someone called the attitude object. An attitude has three major components: *evaluative beliefs* about the object, *feelings* about the object, and *behaviour tendencies* towards the object. Beliefs include facts, opinions and our general knowledge about the object. Feelings include love, hate, like, dislike and similar sentiments. Behavioural tendencies include our inclinations to act in certain ways towards the object – to approach it, avoid it and so on.

These three aspects of an attitude are very often consistent with one another. For example, if we have a positive feeling towards something, we tend to have positive beliefs about it and behave positively towards it. This, however, does not mean that our every action will accurately reflect our attitudes. What is important is to develop strong positive attitudes so that the same are reflected in our behaviour.

Development of attitudes

Man's attitude develops as he develops. But no man's life develops apart from the lives of his fellows. Just as each man's life intersects the lives of others – but only at certain points – and just as each man's life story is similar to – but not identical with – the life stories of his neighbours, so are the attitudes of his family, friends, neighbours and compatriots.

Attitudes develop in the process of 'want satisfaction'

While coping with various problems in trying to satisfy one's wants, the individual develops attitudes. One develops favourable attitudes towards objects and people that satisfy one's wants. An individual will develop unfavourable attitudes towards objects and persons that block the achievement of one's goals.

An individual's attitudes may come to have 'surplus' instrumental value for him/her. He/she develops attitudes in response to problem situations – in trying to satisfy specific wants. In so far as one's attitudes are enduring systems, they remain with one and may be used to solve a number of different problems – to satisfy a number of wants.

Thus one important factor in the formation of attitudes is 'want satisfaction'. Not only do attitudes give meaning to the individual's world, they serve him/her in their attempted achievements of various other goals. Any given attitude may serve various goals, and different wants can give rise to the same enduring attitude.

The attitudes of an individual are shaped by the information to which one is exposed

Attitudes are not only developed in the service of wants; they are also shaped by the information to which an individual is exposed. In order to satisfy one's various wants, an individual develops certain attitudes that help in achieving one's goal. There attitudes will be formed on the basis of whatever facts the individual can gather from various sources. Living in a complex world, one is at the mercy of various authorities for much of the cognitive content of ones attitude. These authorities are sometimes unreliable, through ignorance or intent. In addition the individual may not be able to distinguish between truth and falsehood or between actual and misleading facts and when he/she does pick up facts by themselves, they again run the risk of being fooled. Finally, when one can find no facts, one must, invent 'facts' oneself.

All of this suggests that the incidence of superstitions, delusions and prejudices will be related to the reliability of the authorities we must depend upon (teachers, newspapers, books, telecasts, broadcasts), the range of experiences to which we have been subjected, and the degree to which our major wants are adequately satisfied.

The group affiliations of the individual help determine the formation of his attitudes
The group affiliations of an individual play a vital role in the formation of one's attitudes. Both the membership groups with which an individual affiliates and the non-membership groups to which one aspires to belong are important in shaping one's attitudes.

But an individual does not passively absorb the prevailing attitudes in the various groups with which one affiliates. Attitudes, like cognitions, *develop selectively in the process of want-satisfaction*. An individual will pick and choose among the attitudes offered, those which are want-satisfying. And every individual affiliates with many groups, which may endorse congruent or incongruent attitudes. The effect of group influences on the formation of attitudes is thus indirect and complex.

Do attitudes of the individual reflect his/her personality?

One of the effects of group influences upon attitude development is to produce uniformity of attitudes among the members of various social groups. But in the midst of uniformity there is also diversity. A major factor making for diversity is the existence of personality differences among individuals. Individuals tend to accept those attitudes that complement his/her personality. This is true for such varied attitudes as ethnocentrism, religious attitudes, political attitudes and attitudes towards foreign affairs.

The personality of the individual, however, is not a perfectly integrated system and the individual may take over attitudes that are inconsistent or contradictory because of three reasons: different teachings of his authorities in different areas, conflicting group affiliations and conflicting wants. *Man can and does serve many masters.*

Is your attitude positive?

The following scale is developed by the author to approximately measure the direction of your attitude. Respond to the statements positively or negatively with truthfulness. Remember your honesty is the key to your success.

1. I always take into consideration the feelings of everyone when deciding on matters related with the group. *Yes/No*
2. I am confident that everyone will accept what I decide. *Yes/No*
3. I believe that slow and steady wins the race. *Yes/No*
4. To be humble is to be great. *Yes/No*
5. I can achieve what I dream of. *Yes/No*
6. Everyone has the potential to do anything and everything. *Yes/No*
7. All efforts are always positively rewarded. *Yes/No*
8. All have been born to fulfil a purpose in life. *Yes/No*
9. Gracefully accepting criticism is the key to success. *Yes/No*
10. I strongly believe in the saying that a stitch in time saves nine. *Yes/No*
11. I am always grateful to all for the various goods they have done to me. *Yes/No*

12. I value reading and writing in spare time. *Yes/No*
13. Most of my friends are better than me. *Yes/No*
14. I like the tasks that are assigned to me. *Yes/No*

After you have responded to the above statements give 1 point to the *Yes* responses you have ticked and 0 to the *No* responses you have ticked. If your score lies between 0-4 you have a **negative attitude**; if your score lies between 5-10 your have a **neutral attitude** and if your score lays beyond 11 you have a **positive attitude**.

Developing a positive attitude

Having a positive attitude is very essential for personality development and growth. If you have not positively passed the attitude test do not be disheartened. You can develop a positive attitude. It is easy but requires sincerity and dedication on your part. Your need to achieve will determine your success. So let us move and build our attitude step-by-step. *The steps outlined ahead do not follow any hierarchical order. One and all are important.*

Change your perceptual style

We see the world through our own glasses. We see good and bad. We see beautiful and ugly. But actually what we see is not always reality. We see what we feel from within and what we want to see. Our perceptions reflect what we are from within. Our attitudes, beliefs and feelings force us to look for consistencies in the outside world. Our attention becomes selective and we do not see reality in totality but only segments of things. Such information is not only harmful to ourselves but to others also with whom we interact. We have to learn to view the situation in totality and then only weigh the pros and cons before we form opinions. In short, we have to change our focus of attention. Look at the better side of things and people. We all have our weaknesses but it is our strengths that are of importance. We have to identify and tap our potentials and those of others for effective living.

Count your blessings – name them one by one
Count your blessings and name them one by one and it will surprise you what all has been done by others for you. Mostly we have a tendency to think and list things that others have not done for us. We surely have expectations from others to fulfil our needs but it is not possible for them to fulfil each and every need of ours. We have to place ourselves in their place and then think if it was possible. Children often make unnecessary demands from parents but parents do not always do the needful. It is not that parents do not love their children but they use their discretion, as well as act within their limitations. In the same way, when our demands are not met we should not have a grudge. In fact we should be grateful and thankful for what all has been done for us so far and will be done in the near future. Thus we have to develop an attitude of gratitude.

Moral education is a must — strengthens the superego

Are you literate? Are you educated? These two questions may seem the same to you, but they are not. There is a vast difference between literacy and education. We all may be literate but not educated. Some may be illiterate yet educated. A literate person is one who can read and write. Whereas an educated individual is one who has received mental and moral training.

We have to have morals. Our society does not accept the immoral. We have to educate ourselves with what is morally right. We have to strengthen our superego – which is the internal representative of traditional values and ideas of society and which makes us aware of the right and wrong. Then only will we be able to differentiate right from wrong as well as evaluate ourselves and others.

Develop positive feelings about yourself

In psychological terms feelings about oneself are referred to as *self-esteem*. High self-esteem – a feeling of self-worth – pays dividends. People who feel good about themselves have fewer ulcers and fewer sleepless nights, succumb less easily to pressure, are less likely to use drugs, are more persistent at difficult tasks, and are happier.

People with low self-esteem do not necessarily see themselves as worthless or wicked, but they do lack good things to say about themselves. Such low self-esteem exacts its own costs. More often than not, unhappiness and despair coexist with low self-esteem. People who feel they are falling short of their hopes are vulnerable to depression. Those whose self-image falls short of what they think they ought to be, are vulnerable to anxiety.

Thus it is important for us to appreciate our good points, accept our weaknesses and work upon them. To love oneself is the beginning of a lifelong romance.

Use your discretion

We all have been blessed with the ability to act purposefully, to think rationally and to deal effectively with our environment. We should have a definite purpose and direction in life. Activities, which are misleading but seem attractive, may tempt us into changing our track. However, remember that you have a mission to fulfil and a goal to achieve in life. The temptation may be lovely but you have promises to keep and miles to go before you achieve your goal. You have to think rationally. Reason and understanding are very essential for development of a positive attitude. We have to efficiently manipulate our environment to achieve our goal. We have to use our discretion to judge good and evil. We have to go with the good and try to curb evil on the way.

Love your work

We all have been assigned some work or the other to carry on. We may like this work or not but it has to be done. If we have a negative attitude towards it we will find it

difficult to do. Try to generate interest in it. Try working it out differently. This will not only contribute to your performance but also enhance your creativity. The best strategy to do work which you are not much interested in is trying to do first what is essential, then what is possible and finally you will realise that you are doing the impossible. It is the attitude with which you look into things that acts as a work force behind your doings. *Think positive, do positive.*

A good start is half the battle won
What do you say when you get up in the morning: Oh God! It is morning or Thank God it is morning! The first statement is a pessimistic outlook for the day and the second an optimistic one. How you begin your day is important. Think of all that you have to achieve. Every morning look back at what you did yesterday and then try to beat it. You have to move ahead with your own frame of reference that is healthy for you as well as for others.

You have it in you
Though there is an alpha, there is no omega for developing a positive attitude. An end means it is over. Perfection does not end. It always begins afresh. No individual is perfect. No matter how hard one tries, we are all humans. We try, we achieve but we also fail. But those who stop, lose and those who retry achieve what they could not before. Achieving perfection is a cyclic process that does

not have any end. So keep trying. Do not quit. You have it in you. It is just a matter of time and effort. You will surely achieve near perfection.

Self-Monitoring

People generally know what they are fleeing from but not what they are in search of

Have you ever been in a dilemma as to which group to join? After walking into a roomful of people, your answer may depend on whether you are high or low in *self-monitoring*. The concept of self-monitoring is important to positive thinking and personality development. This refers to how much people monitor (observe, regulate and control) the image of themselves they display to others in public.

Are you in control of your 'self'?

The following self-monitoring scale is designed by the author to approximately measure your self-monitoring behaviour. Respond to each statement, positively or negatively, but honestly. Remember honesty is your key to success.

1. I would probably make a good actor. *Yes/No*
2. I have never been good at games. *Yes/No*
3. I am not always the person I appear to be. *Yes/No*

4. In a group I am rarely the centre of attention. *Yes/No*
5. I guess I put on a show to impress and entertain others. *Yes/No*
6. At a party, I let others keep the jokes and stories going. *Yes/No*
7. I am keenly interested in the actions of others. *Yes/No*
8. I speak my mind out no matter who is listening. *Yes/No*
9. I am flexible and adaptable. *Yes/No*
10. I do not like to be flexible from situation to situation. *Yes/No*
11. I have well-defined roles. *Yes/No*
12. I identify myself in terms of my beliefs, emotions, values and personality. *Yes/No*
13. My friends are mostly knowledgeable in various areas. *Yes/No*
14. All my friends are alike in certain basic ways. *Yes/No*
15. I am highly concerned about my outer appearance. *Yes/No*
16. My wardrobe is less varied. *Yes/No*
17. For a life partner my criterion is beauty. *Yes/No*
18. For a life partner my criterion is personality. *Yes/No*
19. I have the ability to carry on an affair with two people at the same time. *Yes/No*
20. I believe that there is only one real love for a person. *Yes/No*

21. I prefer jobs where my role is very clearly defined. Yes/No
22. I prefer jobs where I can 'just be myself'. Yes/No

Now give a point of 1 to each *Yes* and 0 points to each *No*. Select the odd questions (1, 3, 5, 7, 9, 11, 13, 15, 17, 19, 21) and total their score. This will give you your score against high self-monitoring. Select the even questions (2, 4, 6, 8, 10, 12, 14, 16, 18, 20, 22) and total their score. This will give you your score against low self-monitoring.

High self-monitoring
If your score lies between **0-6** you are **very low** on monitoring; between 7-9 you are **low**; between 10-15 *average*; between 16-18 **high** and between 19-22 you are **very high** on self-monitoring.

Low self-monitoring
If your score lies between 0-6 you are **not a very low** self-monitor; between 7-9 you are **not a low** self-monitor; between 10-15 you are an **average low** self-monitor; between 16-18 you are **high on low** self-monitor and between 19-22 you are **very high on low** self-monitor.

Some of us are *high self-monitors*, who are very sensitive to situations and expectations. High self-monitors like to ask, "Who does this situation want me to be, and how can I be that person?" In contrast, *low self-monitors* are less interested in controlling the impression they make. Such people seek to faithfully express what they really think and feel. It is as if they want to know, "Who am I, and how can I be me in this situation?"

The way people define what they regard as *me* has an impact on their lives and behaviour. Persons high in self-monitoring take a flexible approach to defining themselves. They are very interested in their public image. Low self-monitors, on the other hand, try to accurately present their beliefs and principles no matter what the situation is.

Now that you have measured yourself on the self-monitoring scale, its time to know yourself better. Detailed ahead are the characteristics of high and low self-monitors.

Characteristics of self-monitors

High self-monitors

They are keenly interested in the actions of others and in trying to 'read' their motives, attitudes and traits. Presumably, high self-monitors do this so that they will know how to present themselves to a particular person, such as a date. They are also flexible and adaptable. High self-monitors tend to declare who they are by listing their roles and memberships. They choose friends who are skilled or knowledgeable in various areas. They also tend to have specific friends for specific activities. They are concerned with outer appearances and choose their clothes, hairstyle, jewellery, and so forth, to project an image. They select their partner on the basis of outward appearance. They believe it is possible to love two people at the same time. People high on self-monitoring prefer jobs where their role is very clearly defined.

Low self-monitors

Persons low on self-monitoring seek to match their public behaviour to their private attitudes, feelings and beliefs. They tend to speak their mind no matter who is listening. They rarely change from situation to situation. They value a match between who they believe they are and what they do. Low self-monitors do not want to change opinions to please others or win their favour. They identify themselves in terms of their beliefs, emotions, values and personality. Their friends will generally be alike in basic traits. No matter what the activity, they prefer to go together with the same friends. They have a wardrobe that is less varied; they do not have to look different as often as high self-monitors do. When choosing a partner they place importance on personality. Persons low on self-monitoring believe that there is only one real love for a person. In the job field they prefer jobs where they can 'just' be themselves.

Implications

As you can see, there are advantages and disadvantages to being either high or low in self-monitoring. In general, high self-monitors are adaptable and present themselves well in social situations. However, they tend to reveal little about their private feelings, beliefs and intentions. In addition to this, a discrepancy between their attitudes and actions may have a negative effect on relationships.

The primary drawback of being low in self-monitoring is a tendency to be unresponsive to the demands of different situations. Low self-monitors want to 'just be themselves', even when adjustments in self-presentation would make them more effective.

One true self

Is there a single 'true self' that underlies the many roles we play in daily life? High self-monitors, in particular, act as if they have many selves. For these people, controlling the image they impart is a way of life, at parties, in meetings, in classes, and elsewhere. The 'public self' of high self-monitors may or may not be backed by a perceived 'real me' on the inside. In many cases, it may be better to try to understand the *self in action* by looking at the ways people define themselves. Just as the answer to the question "Who am I?" varies for each person, the answer to the question "Do I have a single true self?" may also vary.

Do you have a single true self? Give this question some thought. The answer to this question is important for developing positive thinking and thereby personality development.

Another important and related concept is that of *self-image*. It refers to the total subjective perception we have of our own body and personality. Much of our behaviour can be understood as an attempt to maintain consistency between our self-image and our actions. Experiences that match the self-image are admitted to consciousness and contribute a gradual change in the self. Information or feelings inconsistent with the self-image are said to be incongruent. It is incongruent, for example, to think of yourself as a considerate person if others frequently mention your rudeness. It is also incongruent to pretend you are kind when you are feeling callous or to say you are not angry when you are seething inside.

Experiences seriously incongruent with the self-image can be threatening and they are often distorted or denied conscious recognition. Blocking, denying or distorting experiences prevents the self from changing. This creates a gulf between the self-image and reality. As the self-image grows more unrealistic, the incongruent person becomes confused, vulnerable, dissatisfied or seriously maladjusted. Recent studies have confirmed that people who know themselves well tend to like and feel good about themselves. Poor self-knowledge is associated with low self-esteem.

When your self-image is consistent with what you really think, feel, do and experience, you are best able to actualise your potentials. It is also essential to have congruence between the self-image and the *ideal self*. The ideal self is an idealised image of oneself. It is the image of the person you would most like to be.

Research has shown that people with a close match between their self-image and ideal self tend to be socially poised, confident and resourceful. Those with a poor match tend to be depressed, anxious, insecure and lacking in social skills. Thus our self-image can greatly influence our thinking and personality.

Possible selves

Trying on one's self for size

Your ideal self is only one of the many personal identities you may have pondered. Each of us harbours images of many *possible selves*. These selves include the person we would most like to become (the ideal self), as well as other selves we could become or are afraid of becoming.

Possible selves translate our hopes, fears, fantasies and goals into specific images of who we could be. For eg, when a lawyer begins his/her career, he/she might picture himself as a successful attorney; a husband in a troubled marriage might picture himself as a divorcee; and a person on a diet might imagine both slim and grossly obese possible selves. Such self-images tend to direct future behaviour. They also give meaning to current behaviour and help us evaluate it. For example, the unhappy spouse might be moved by upsetting images of his 'divorced self' to try saving his marriage.

Possible selves may guide even day-to-day decisions. Purchasing clothes, a car, cologne, membership in a health club and the like, may be influenced by images of a valued future self. Of course, identities are not all equally possible. Almost everyone, 30 years and above have probably felt the anguish of realising that some cherished possible selves will never be realised. But this should not dishearten you because it is from here where you start thinking in the positive. Where there is a will there is a way.

Achiever's Profile – Do You Have It in You?

Destiny is not a matter of chance, it is a matter of choice; it is not a thing to be waited for, it is a thing to be achieved

I really want others to be appreciative of me, admire me and respect the person I am. I have to move towards achieving this objective. To achieve this target you have to initiate, sustain and direct your thinking in this direction. This will provide you an internal energy that will energise your behaviour. These motivated activities will be the beginning of creating a *need for achievement*. This need will cause a psychological state or feeling called a *drive*, to develop. This drive will activate a *response* designed to attain your *goal* that will satisfy your need for becoming the perfect individual you always wanted to be.

The need for achievement is the desire to meet your individual standard of excellence. A housewife, carpenter, clerk or student could live creatively and make full use of his or her potentials. Persons with high need for achievement strive to do well in any situation in which evaluation takes place.

The tendency of making full use of one's potentials is referred to as *self-actualisation*. It is the process of fully developing personal potentials. One who is living creatively and making full use of his or her potentials is a *self-actualiser*.

Where you stand is very important to know for you to act in accordance. So you must test yourself first.

This test is designed by the author to measure approximately the self-actualiser in you. Respond honestly to the questions positively or negatively. Remember your honesty is the key to your success.

1. Do you have the ability to judge situations correctly and honestly? *Yes/No*
2. Are you sensitive to the fake and dishonest? *Yes/No*
3. Do you accept your human nature with all its shortcomings? *Yes/No*
4. Do you accept the shortcomings of others as well as the contradictions of the human condition with humour and tolerance? *Yes/No*
5. Do you extend your creativity into everyday activities? *Yes/No*
6. Are you usually enthusiastic, engaged and spontaneous? *Yes/No*
7. Do you have a mission to fulfil in life? *Yes/No*
8. Do you have some task or problem outside of your own? *Yes/No*
9. Are you free from dependency on external authority or other people? *Yes/No*
10. Are you resourceful and independent? *Yes/No*
11. Do you constantly renew appreciation of life's basic goods? *Yes/No*

12. Do you have an 'innocence of vision' like that of an artist or child? Yes/No
13. Do you feel a sense of deep identification with others? Yes/No
14. Do you feel a sense of deep identification with the human situation in general? Yes/No
15. Are your interpersonal relationships marked by deep, loving bonds? Yes/No
16. Do you have the capacity to laugh at yourself? Yes/No
17. Do you make jokes that do not hurt others? Yes/No
18. Do you have marked feelings of ecstasy, harmony and deep meaning? Yes/No
19. Do you feel as one with the universe? Yes/No
20. Do you feel safe? Yes/No
21. Are you relaxed? Yes/No
22. Do others accept you? Yes/No
23. Do others love you? Yes/No
24. Are you loving and alive? Yes/No

Now rate yourself. For every **Yes**, give 1 point and for every *No* 0. Total up the points. If you score between 0-6 you are a **very low** self-actualiser; 7-9 you are a **low** self-actualiser; 10-15 you are **average**; 16-20 you are a **high** actualiser and 21-24 you are a **very high** self-actualiser.

Abraham Maslow's whole characteristics of self-actualising people: A bird's-eye view

1. They have more efficient perceptions of reality and are more comfortable with it.

2. They accept themselves and their own natures almost without thinking about it.
3. Their behaviour is marked by simplicity and naturalness and by lack of artificiality or straining for effect.
4. They focus on problems outside themselves; they are concerned with basic issues and eternal questions.
5. They like privacy and tend to be detached.
6. They have relative independence of their physical and social environments; they rely on their own development and continued growth.
7. They do not take blessings for granted, but appreciate, again and again, the basic pleasures of life.
8. They experience limitless horizons and the intensification of any 'unself-conscious' experience often of a mystical type.
9. They have a deep feeling of kingship with others.
10. They develop deep ties with a few other self-actualising individuals.
11. They are democratic in a deep sense. Although not indiscriminate, they are not really aware of differences.
12. They are strongly ethical, with definite moral standards, though their attitudes are conventional; they relate to ends rather than means.
13. Their humour is real and related to philosophy, not hostility. They tend to be more serious and thoughtful.

14. They are original and inventive, less constricted and fresher than others.
15. While they tend to be inclined towards the conventional and exist well within the culture, they live by the law of their own characters rather than those of society.
16. They experience imperfections and have emotional responses like others.

Qualities of self-actualisers

The test you went through and its results thereafter must have made clear the distance you stand from being a self-actualiser. The test was designed to measure the following qualities found common in self-actualisers the world over:

Efficient perceptions of reality

Self-actualisers are able to judge situations correctly and honestly and are sensitive to the fake and dishonest.

Comfortable acceptance of self and other's nature

They accept their human nature with all its shortcomings. The shortcomings of other's and contradictions of the human conditions are also accepted by them with humour and tolerance.

Spontaneity

They extend their creativity into everyday activities. They tend to be usually alive, engaged and spontaneous.

Prioritising/Prioritise tasks
They have a mission to fulfil in life or some task or problem outside of themselves to pursue.

Autonomy
They are free from dependence on external authority or other people. They tend to be resourceful and independent.

Continued appreciation
The self-actualisers constantly renew appreciation of life's basic goods. They have an 'innocence of vision' like that of an artist or child.

Fellowship with humanity
Self-actualisers feel a deep identification with others and the human situation in general.

Profound interpersonal relationships
The interpersonal relationships of self-actualisers are marked by deep, loving bonds.

Non-hostile sense of humour
They have a wonderful capacity to laugh at themselves. They never make a joke that will intentionally hurt someone.

Peak experiences
Self-actualisers have frequent occurrences of peak experiences. These are marked by feelings of ecstasy, harmony and deep meaning. They feel at one with the universe, stronger and calmer than ever before, filled with light, beauty and goodness. In short, they feel safe, non-anxious, accepted, loved, loving and alive.

How to move towards self-actualisation
If you have failed the test you need not get disheartened. This book is meant especially for you. If you have passed you still need to know.

There is no magic formula for leading a more creative life. Self-actualisation is primarily a *process*, not a goal or an end point. As such, it requires hardwork, patience, and commitment on your part. Here are some ways to begin.

- **Be willing to change** – Begin by asking yourself, "Am I living in a way that is deeply satisfying to me and which truly expresses me?" If not, be prepared to make changes in your life. Indeed, ask yourself this question often and accept the need for continual change.
- **Take responsibility** – You can become an architect of self by acting as if you are personally responsible for every aspect of your life. Shouldering responsibility in this way helps end the habit of blaming others for your own shortcomings.
- **Examine your motives** – Self-discovery involves an element of risk. If most of your behaviour seems to be directed by a desire for safety or security, it may be time to test the limits of these needs. Try to make each decision a choice for growth, not a response to fear or anxiety.
- **Experience honestly and directly** – Wishful thinking is another barrier to personal growth. Self-actualisers trust themselves enough to accept all kinds of information without distorting it to fit their

fears and desires. Try to see yourself as others do. Be willing to admit, "I was wrong" or "I failed because I was irresponsible."
- **Make use of positive experiences** – You should actively repeat activities that have caused feelings of awe, amazement, exaltation, renewal, reverence, humility, fulfilment or joy.
- **Be prepared to be different** – Everyone has the potential for 'greatness', but most fear of becoming what they might. As part of personal growth, be prepared to trust your own impulses and feelings; do not automatically judge yourself by the standards of others. Accept your uniqueness.
- **Get involved** – Get personally involved and committed. Turn your attention to problems outside yourself.
- **Maintain an average level of anxiety** – Research has emphasised the constructive contribution of anxiety to the growth of the self. It is maintained that *self-actualisation*, the creative use of one's talents, comes about only through encounters with anxiety-provoking experiences. New possibilities for overcoming potential threats are said to enlarge the scope of one's activity and to increase personal freedom.
- **Assess your progress** – Since there is no final point at which one becomes self-actualised, it is important to gauge your progress frequently and to renew your efforts. If you feel bored at school,

at a job, or in a relationship, consider it a challenge or an indication that you have not taken responsibility for personal growth. Almost any activity can be used as a chance for self-enhancement if it is approached creatively.

How Positively Do You Think?

Do what you can, with what you have, where you are

It is time to really test your thinking. Given below are a few statements. You are required to read them and respond to them positively or negatively. Be honest with yourself.
1. There are people who are much better than I am. *Yes/No*
2. I always want things to be done my way. *Yes/No*
3. I firmly believe that the first impression is the last impression. *Yes/No*
4. I do not make hasty decisions. *Yes/No*
5. I lack faith in abilities. *Yes/No*
6. I welcome healthy criticism from others. *Yes/No*
7. I never do backbiting. *Yes/No*
8. I am known to crack jokes at the cost of others. *Yes/No*
9. I wish I could have been more handsome/ beautiful. *Yes/No*
10. I patiently listen when others are talking. *Yes/No*
11. Most of my problems do not seem to have solutions. *Yes/No*

12. My mind is clear of polluted thoughts. *Yes/No*
13. A chance lost is lost forever. *Yes/No*
14. I am straightforward and honest. *Yes/No*
15. Creativity is only for the builders, developers and artists. *Yes/No*
16. I strongly believe that I am indispensable. *Yes/No*
17. I have a high opinion about myself. *Yes/No*
18. I hold respect for all class of people. *Yes/No*
19. I am always right in what I say and do. *Yes/No*
20. I like to take up new challenges. *Yes/No*
21. I trust every decision I take. *Yes/No*
22. I do not like to take additional responsibilities. *Yes/No*
23. Making lame excuses is an art that not everyone can master. *Yes/No*
24. I always think twice before I act. *Yes/No*
25. I always speak positive about myself. *Yes/No*
26. I seldom speak positive about others. *Yes/No*
27. My heart rules over my head. *Yes/No*
28. I do not have many good things to say about myself. *Yes/No*
29. I can achieve what I dream of. *Yes/No*
30. All efforts are mostly positively rewarded. *Yes/No*
31. Gracefully accepting criticism is the key to success. *Yes/No*
32. I complain when things are not done in my favour. *Yes/No*

After you have marked your responses give 1 point each to the *Yes* you have ticked against question no's. 1, 4, 6, 7, 10, 12, 14, 17, 18, 20, 21, 24, 25, 29, 30 and 31 and

1 point each for the *No* ticked against question no's. 2, 3, 5, 8, 9, 11, 13, 15, 16, 19, 22, 23, 26, 27, 28 and 32. Thereafter total your score for both. If you have scored between 27-32 you have **high** positive thinking. Between 20-26 **you have average** positive thinking. Between 13-19 it is **neutral**. Between 7-12 it is **negative** and between 0-6 it is **very negative**.

If you are a positive thinker, it is well and good. But if not, you can be one. The only thing you need is a desire to think positive.

How to develop positive thought?

Think like a man of action, act like a man of thought. Man is always born free yet everywhere he finds himself in bondage. He is bound by what his parent's think of him and expect him to do. He is bound by the expectations of society. He is bound by religious thought and philosophy. He is bound by what others think. In short he is bound by everything that matters. We have to free ourselves from bondage. We have to free ourselves from within. We have to evolve as independent thinkers. If we cannot have independent thoughts we cannot develop our '*self*' into a better one. However, even though being independent, our thought should take into consideration not one but all humans and animals who coexist with us. So let us begin to develop and expand our horizons as independent thinkers.

The points given ahead do not follow any hierarchical order. They are just guidelines for developing positive thought. Positive thought is infinite and it goes on and on.

Constantly indulge in self-evaluation

We are generally inclined to believe what we are not because it satisfies our ego. People say flattering things about us and we believe them. Generally most of us only think thing's worth believing in if its hard to believe. But we have to critically evaluate ourselves. We have to know our good as well as our bad qualities. We have to work upon the weak ones and improvise them. We are what we are and we have to strive to be what we want to be. So keep indulging in honest and critical self-evaluation. This self-evaluation will pave the way for you towards positive thinking.

Accept reality

Truth is always stranger than fiction and truth cannot be denied. It is and will always remain as truth. We must accept the truth as we cannot evade it. Denial of reality may give temporary relief but later on it will cause us psychological problems. This is not good for our mental health. So why go around playing hide and seek. Accept what is there and live with it. Harry Truman has rightly commented, "*I never give them hell. I just tell the truth, and they think it is hell.*" So let the truth not be hell for you. Let it prevail.

Accept others as they are

People differ on all dimensions and our assessment of them should take this into consideration. I am I, and you are you. You cannot be me and I cannot be you. But together we make up the society. There has to be a harmony in discord. Learn to accept others as they are and you will find acceptance in return.

Evaluate behaviour within situational framework
One's behaviour is largely the outcome of the stimulation one receives from the immediate environment. While evaluating one's behaviour we should take this into consideration. Many an action may be justified in a given situation. Place yourself in someone else's shoes and then think how you would have behaved under the same prevailing circumstances. Maybe you will be able to form more positive opinions about other peoples' behaviours.

Develop confidence in yourself and your abilities
Lacking confidence leads to inferiority complex. We tend to give up even before we try. Do what you can, with what you have and where you are. Start with what is possible and you will slowly end up doing the impossible. Everything is possible to achieve if one has a will to do so. So develop confidence in yourself and have faith in your abilities.

Do not look down upon others
Do not ever think yourself to be superior to anyone. A superior exists because an inferior is there. If you look down upon others it generates within you the idea of superiority. This in turn leads to you feeling inferior to many. White is white and black is black because there is a white and a black. So never generate the feelings of superiority in your outlook towards yourself or else you too will be inferior to many others. The more noble a person is, the harder it is for him to think inferior of others.

Respect the abilities of others
The way to get things done is not to mind who gets the credit of doing them. We should identify and respect people's abilities and use their potentials to the best of their as well as our advantage.

Welcome and appreciate healthy criticism
It is very easy to criticise others but very difficult to accept when others criticise us. Criticism acts as a guiding and motivating force for us. It helps us to perform even better and move ahead. If we are only appreciated for our doings then this indicates that we have stagnated. So learn to take criticism gracefully and do things even better.

Do not indulge in backbiting
One must not stab people in the back. This is a habit of cowards. Be bold and express your feelings before the concerned person. It will make you feel better and do him/her good too.

Appreciate your physical being
'Beauty lies in the eye of the beholder' and 'A thing of beauty is a joy forever' are two very common but widely misinterpreted sayings. Beauty does not only imply your outward being, it is also your inner self. What is beautiful within is a joy forever. I am a very lean and thin guy and many people out of the way comment on it. My reply to them is – "It is your problem not mine since it is bothering you not me. I know who and what I am." So learn to appreciate your physical being. It is God's gift to you.

Pay attention when others speak
Most of us are in a habit of not listening when others are speaking. We always try to push and lay our views. It is very important that we be patient listeners because we learn a lot more than we actually know. This will even help us gauge the thoughts and feelings of others, which in turn will help them understand better.

Remember there is a solution to every problem
A problem exists because a solution for the same is there. Without a solution a problem has no existence of its own. It is when things get complicated they turn into problems. Try different methods and approaches in trying to solve your problems. Flexibility is the master key to solutions. Do not give up on problem solving tasks. You surely will succeed.

Devote time to constructive work
It is well said that an empty mind is a devil's workshop. Spend your free time doing constructive things. It will also enhance your creativity. Creativity leads to innovation and you will find yourself moving towards self-actualisation.

Clear your mind of polluted thoughts
Purity of mind, body and soul are essential components of positive thinking. Hear no evil, see no evil and speak no evil. Notice the difference it makes.

Life is an experience, enjoy it
Life is like the spectrum, which has various colours, but together they look beautiful. Take life as it comes to you. All is for some good or the other. We live and think only in the present context. This does not always

produce fruitful results for our future. Things that are not acceptable to us today may have good consequences for us in the future. So experience every shade of life as it comes to you and learn to enjoy it. After all we only live once.

There is always a second chance

People fret over missed chances and opportunities. Fretting is not going to help you. Even if you would have got the chance you still could not have predicted your exact future. No one has seen tomorrow. Maybe there is something better waiting for you to come. I firmly believe in the divine will and wish and quote it here, "*I have learnt to wait patiently for HIS will to unfold, for he has in store blessings untold.*" Things happen for the better most of the time. There is no use crying over spilt milk.

Be honest and appreciate honesty

Honesty has always been the best policy. Honesty is not only a term related with financial matters it covers the entire domain of human character. Be honest with yourself first and honesty with others will follow.

Learn to accept your mistakes

A man who makes no mistakes does not usually make anything. There are three types of people. In the first category are those who say, " I am always right and others are always wrong." In the second one are those who say "I am always wrong" and finally we have those who say, "I am at times right and at times wrong." Try to be the last types. Owing up to our mistakes is greatness on our part and it also helps clear our conscious of guilt.

Express yourself

Expression of feelings is the key to a good mental health. Feelings are never wrong. They are the reflection of your honesty within. Bottled up feelings weigh us down and we start behaving in unnatural ways. So give vent to your feelings taking the situation and circumstances into consideration. It is always good to express ourselves as it gives us more space within for generation of fresh and healthy feelings.

Do not let your heart rule your head

Think and then think again. Is it really what you had thought? Let your behaviour be thought-oriented and not a resultant emotion.

Accept challenges

Destiny is not a matter of chance, it is a matter of choice; it is not a thing to be waited for, it is a thing to be achieved. So do not run away from tough situations. Go ahead and take it up.

Avoid dependency

Learn to be independent. Independent in thought, word and deed. Unless and until you learn to trust yourself you cannot trust others. So let go of any clinging attitude you have. Grow and let grow.

Do not make lame excuses

Many people are in a habit of making lame excuses for justifying their acts. The chains of such a habit is too weak to be felt until it gets too strong to be broken. So watch out before its too late. Making lame excuses will not help you develop and grow. Accept the truth and responsibility rather than making excuses.

Be kind to others

An act of kindness, no matter how small, is never wasted. There is an old saying that God helps those who help themselves, but I do not fully agree with this. I believe that *God helps those who help others*. So go out of your way to help people in need and experience the satisfaction and happiness it brings to you.

You are not indispensable

Never have the wrong notion that you are indispensable. Accept the fact that there have been and there are people better than you in every field. If you start thinking of yourself to be indispensable, it is the end of the road for you. Give room to yourself as well as others to grow. Accepting this will make you strive ahead rather than stagnate yourself.

Do not indulge in flattery

People who flatter are the most dangerous of human species. They seldom have favourable opinions about the one they are flattering. People flatter for the sole purpose of obtaining favours. Such people seldom speak good behind the back of the one they flatter. So never encourage or believe flatterers and never indulge in flattery. A word for flatterers *"Do not try to tell me what I am because I know what I am not."*

Remember one never loses

If you have ventured into some work and you fail to achieve the desired results do not ever think that you have lost. Evaluate the whole situation. Find out where you had faltered and try and rectify it. Thus you have learned and learning is never a loss. You have only gained.

Always talk positive

A man is known by his language. Try to avoid using negative words. The order of the words one selects tells a lot about the individual's thought process. If the language is complex it indicates about the complexity of the individual. Ambiguity in language must be avoided. Statements must reflect and have a positive thought content. While talking follow the SAAD principle: Simple, Active, Affirmative and Declarative. Use words and statements that are simple, grammatically active, affirmative and declarative. Think positive and talk positive.

Be infinitely positive

Mathematically even two negatives make up a positive. There is no end to positive thought and deeds. All the good in this world is positive. All the bad in this world also has a positive side. We have to seek the good. If we do this then anything evil on its own will be eradicated. So let us always think of the brighter side of life.

I would like to sum up by quoting Theodore Roosevelt – *This world will not be a good place for any of us to live in unless we make it a good place for all of us to live in.*

I hope by going through this book you must have come to know your *self* better. You have the potential and will always have it. All of it is lurking inside you. It is basically your thinking which will enable you to develop your personality. I wish you all the best once again. Go get it out from within and give the best of yourself to the world. It is truly said – *For it is in giving that we receive.*